"*Lewis and Clark's Illinois Volunteers* emphasizes the significant role the Illinois Country had in the success of the Expedition. It should be required reading for every student of Illinois history."
  - Harry K. Windland, treasurer of the Illinois
    Lewis and Clark Bicentennial Commission

"*Lewis and Clark's Illinois Volunteers* is an easy, entertaining read full of assorted tidbits of information about the Illinois cast of characters that accompanied Lewis and Clark on the Corps of Discovery. From the resourceful George Drouillard, dedicated to the very end, to John Newman, at times mutinous, at times commendable, the volunteers are fleshed out with all their virtues and vices for the delight of the reader."
  - Larry Underwood, author of *Guns, Gold and
    Glory, The Custer Fight* and many other books
    on Western Americana

Lewis and Clark's Illinois Volunteers

John and Susan Dunphy

In the Spirit of Lewis & Clark –

[signed] John J. Dunphy

Second Reading Publications: Alton, Illnois.

Second Reading Publications
16 East Broadway
Alton, Illinois 62002
618-462-2830
info@secondreadingbookshop.com

ISBN: 0-9741642-0-8

1st Trade Publication

Introduction

The authors and photographer wish to express their appreciation to Harry Windland, treasurer of the Illinois Lewis and Clark Bicentennial Commission, who suggested to us that a book about the Illinois volunteers of the Corps of Discovery needed to be written. We are also grateful for his kind offer to read our manuscript before it went to press. Larry Underwood, one of America's finest authors of Western Americana, read our pre-publication manuscript as well, and we thank him. Finally, we would like to thank Louis Launer and Sue Zahra of the Metro East Writers Workshop and Michael Murphy, who also critiqued our manuscript.

We wish to acknowledge the cooperation of Father Gerald Hechenberger, pastor of Holy Family Church in Cahokia, Illinois, for allowing us to photograph that beautiful old church; Mary Michals, audio-visual curator of the Illinois State Historical Library, permitted us to photograph the Cahokia Courthouse; Tim Schweizer of the Illinois Department of Natural Resources authorized us to photograph Fort Massac in southern Illinois; Bradley Winn, site manager of the Lewis and Clark State Historic Site, allowed us to photograph the Lewis and Clark Interpretative Center at Hartford, Illinois; Charles James III gave us the green light to photograph the reconstructed Camp River Dubois at Wood River, Illinois; and Marion Sperling of the Madison County Historical Society, who gave us information on the location of the pioneer settlement of Goshen. Thank you one and all!

Finally, we wish to thank our family and friends for their support and encouragement.   We dedicate this book to you.

About the authors:

John J. Dunphy has written articles for national and regional magazines and newspapers for over twenty years. He is the founder of the Metro East Writers Workshop of Greater St. Louis and teaches writing at Lewis and Clark Community College.

Susan Dunphy has worked in research for years and enjoys history. Her articles have appeared in national and regional newspapers for over fifteen years.

Carriy Caylen has been working in the photography industry for several years. She has produced her own line of greeting cards and bookmarks. Caylen does all her own stock photography, which made her the ideal candidate for this book.

Table of Contents

The Beginning

When Thomas Jefferson became president in 1801, he appointed Meriwether Lewis as his private secretary. A lieutenant in the U.S. Army and an accomplished woodsman, Lewis possessed a solid knowledge of America's western frontier: the Indiana Territory.

President Jefferson instructed Lewis to study botany, zoology, geography, ethnology and celestial navigation. The president then secretly appealed to Congress in 1802 to fund an expedition to the Pacific Ocean that Lewis would lead. The following year Lewis began recruiting volunteers for this expedition, designated the Corps of Discovery.

Jefferson hoped Lewis would find "the Northwest Passage," a waterway that stretched to the Pacific Ocean. He also wanted to learn more about the great expanse of land known as the Louisiana Purchase, which the United States acquired from France in 1803, and to establish trade with the tribes of Native Americans who inhabited it.

Lewis, who was promoted to the rank of captain, asked William Clark, a former soldier with whom he had served, to co-command the expedition with him. Although promised the rank of captain, Clark's commission was that of only a second lieutenant. Still, Clark was addressed as captain by Lewis and treated as his equal throughout the journey. The Corps of Discovery's volunteers were not even aware of the disparity in their ranks and knew both men only as captains.

In a letter dated July 2, 1803, Secretary of War Henry Dearborn wrote Lewis to authorize him to call on the commanding officers of Fort Massac and Fort Kaskaskia, both located in the future state of Illinois, to recruit volunteers for the expedition. The letter noted that Lewis could acquire no more than twelve non-commissioned officers and privates as volunteers. In addition, Lewis was permitted to engage the services of an interpreter to accompany the Corps of Discovery.

Dearborn also sent letters to Captain Daniel Bissell, commander at Fort Massac, and his brother, Captain Russell Bissell, commander at Fort Kaskaskia as well as to Captain Amos Stoddard, the commander of an artillery company stationed at Kaskaskia. These letters ordered them to detach any men who might wish to volunteer for the expedition.

The saga began in August 1803 as Lewis left Pittsburgh by keelboat, which was the standard type of vessel for traversing inland waters in the early years of the nineteenth century. Clark joined him at Clarksville, Indiana Territory, and they journeyed down the Ohio River toward their destination: Fort Massac.

Established by the French as Fort Ascension in 1757 to guard against attacks by the British and Native Americans, the fort had been renamed Massiac a few years later. It was abandoned by the French in 1764 shortly before British troops arrived at the site.

The British allowed the fort to deteriorate, and it was captured by the Americans in 1778. Renamed Fort Massac, the site was rebuilt in 1794 as a defense against attacks by Native Americans and the British. It became a port-of-entry for commerce and trade in 1799.

Fort Massac temporarily closed in 1801 but reopened a year later under Captain Daniel Bissell's command. It could hold a company of about 50 men. The fort was made of pickets arranged to form a square with a small bastion at each angle surrounded by about 60 acres of cleared forest.

Fort Massac became Lewis and Clark's initial area of recruitment in Illinois. Their first selection was George Drouillard, an interpreter, followed by two privates: Joseph Whitehouse and John Newman.

2 George Drouillard

Pierre Drouillard, the French-Canadian father of George Drouillard, was a British subject who lived in Detroit. He served the British as an interpreter. George's mother, whose name remains unrecorded, was a Shawnee Native American. In 1776, Pierre married Angelique Deschamps, by whom he fathered several children.

Since George's year of birth remains unknown, it is uncertain whether Pierre fathered him before or during his marriage to Angelique. In any event, it appears that Angelique accepted young George as her stepson and even ensured that he received enough schooling to enable him to read, write and cypher.

While still a youth, George migrated to Cape Girardeau. He later went to Fort Massac and began his career as a professional hunter. Lewis's journal entry for November 11, 1803 noted that he arrived at Fort Massac and engaged "Drewyer," whose name was consistently misspelled in all the explorers' journals, as an interpreter. Drouillard's name was added to the Corp of Discovery roster on January 1, 1804 as "George Druiller." Lewis's first assignment to Drouillard was to dispatch him to Tennessee to pick up eight volunteers for the Corps of Discovery, all of whom proved unsuitable.

Drouillard was the chief hunter on the expedition, and he kept the men well-supplied with freshly-killed game. Paradoxically, he sometimes "adopted" young wild animals, such as beaver and even bear cubs, as pets!

He also served as an interpreter who used sign language to

communicate with the various Native Americans encountered by the Corps of Discovery. Time and time again Drouillard successfully engaged in a variety of other roles when the occasion demanded it. Lewis referred to him in his journal as an excellent man, and with considerable justification.

It was George Drouillard who located lost or stolen horses, gelded horses, took a hand at steering a pirogue on the Columbia River and bartered for canoes at Fort Clatsop. Whenever Lewis set out on an excursion during the expedition, he invariably selected the resourceful Drouillard as one of the men to accompany him.

When Moses B. Reed and Joseph Barter (also known as La Liberte) deserted from the Corps of Discovery, Drouillard was dispatched to find them. Reed was delivered back to camp while La Liberte was apprehended but escaped custody. It was one of Drouillard's few failures while serving with Lewis and Clark.

Drouillard often encountered danger on the expedition. One night he, along with Lewis, Clark, Charbonneau and Sacajawea, were aroused from sleep by a sentinel just in time for them to move the teepee in which they'd been sleeping to safety. The top of a tall tree that had caught fire collapsed on the spot where the teepee had been.

At the Great Falls of the Missouri, this hunter-marksman killed a grizzly bear that was closing in on him from 20 feet with a single bullet. On another occasion, Drouillard's rifle was stolen by a Shoshone Indian. Drouillard rode after him in hot pursuit and, upon catching up with the thief, wrestled the rifle away from him.

Drouillard was also capable of diplomacy when the situation demanded it. A Native American stole a tomahawk that had belonged to Charles Floyd, the only member of the Corps of Discovery to die during the expedition. Clark had intended to present the weapon to Floyd's parents as a memento.

The thief later sold the tomahawk to another Native American, who regarded it as his rightful property and didn't wish to return it to Clark. The tomahawk's new owner was mortally ill and wanted to have it buried with him. Drouillard was able to negotiate the tomahawk's return to Clark in exchange for a handkerchief, two strands of beads and two horses that were to be killed at the grave of the Native American.

Drouillard lived in Cape Girardeau, Missouri for a few years after the expedition. He bought the land grants of Collins and Whitehouse, which he later sold with some additional property for the then-considerable sum of $1,300 in April 1807. But the lure of the wilderness was too strong. Drouillard returned to the life he loved best: trapping, hunting and exploration.

That same year, in a partnership with Manuel Lisa and Benito Vasquez, he established the first American trading post on the Upper Missouri. The post was known variously as Fort Lisa, Fort Manuel, Manuel's Fort and Fort Raymond. Drouillard's role involved locating beaver grounds, trapping, hunting and encouraging Native Americans to bring their pelts to the fort.

Drouillard pursued a deserter from this expedition named Antoine Bissonnette that Lisa had ordered him to bring in dead or alive. Drouillard shot Bissonnette while apprehending him. Lisa procured a canoe to return the wounded man to St. Charles, but he died in the canoe the next day.

Upon returning to St. Louis in early August 1808, Drouillard was arrested for Bissonnette's murder. A trial was held on September 23, and the jury needed just 15 minutes to return a verdict of not guilty. Although a free man again, Drouillard worried that the murder accusation had brought shame on his family and wrote them to express his concern.

Drouillard embarked in the spring of 1809 on another fur-trading expedition under Lisa to start a trading post at the Three Forks of the Missouri River. In March of 1810, Drouillard was one of 32 men who set out from Lisa's Fort to accomplish this mission. They managed to establish the post about a month later on a neck of land between the Jefferson and Madison rivers, approximately two miles above their confluence.

The expedition angered the Blackfoot Nation by trading with enemy tribes and building their post on enemy land. After several close calls and the slaying of some trappers, the expedition decided there was safety in numbers. A party of 21 men left the fort in May to trap.

Drouillard criticized this arrangement as unprofitable and urged the men to set out in smaller parties. One day he announced that he would go up river alone if necessary to ensure more efficient trapping. When asked by the men whether he feared attack by Indians, he replied that his half-Shawnee blood made him too much of an Indian to be caught by Indians.

True to his word, he embarked upon at least one solo trapping trip and returned with many pelts. Another morning he ventured forth with two members of the Delaware tribe. He never returned.

A search party found the two Delaware dead. Drouillard's body and dead horse were about 150 yards away from theirs. He had been decapitated, his entrails torn out and his body hacked to pieces.

The circular pattern of horse tracks suggested that Drouillard had fought the attacking Native Americans while mounted on his horse. He had been armed with a rifle, pistol, knife and tomahawk but had been overwhelmed by his enemy's superior numbers.

3

Joseph Whitehouse

Joseph Whitehouse was born in Virginia about 1775. His family migrated to Kentucky in the 1780s, where he grew up. The journals of Lewis and Clark refer to him as a tailor, and he was often employed in that role to mend the volunteers' clothing. On Christmas Day 1805, Whitehouse gave Clark a pair of moccasins that he had made. An entry for July 7, 1805 noted that Whitehouse was making leather clothes for the men.

Whitehouse kept a journal during his service with the Corps of Discovery, and a number of the entries provide interesting glimpses into the expedition's experiences. When the party's white pirogue almost sank on a stretch of the Missouri River, Whitehouse noted that some papers and nearly all books brought along by the commanders got wet but were not completely spoiled.

Whitehouse endured his share of perils with the Corps of Discovery. He suffered such severe frostbite while hunting at Fort Mandan that he was unable to walk. He was returned to the fort on horseback.

His closest brush with death probably occurred while the expedition was exploring the Three Forks of the Missouri River. The canoe in which Whitehouse had been riding was upset. He was thrown into the river, and another canoe passed over him while he was submerged. Lewis speculated that, had the water been only two inches shallower, the injured Whitehouse would have been crushed to death by the other canoe.

Upon completing the expedition, Whitehouse sold his land warrant of 160 acres to Drouillard for $240. In 1807, a St. Louis court ordered Whitehouse arrested for debt. He rejoined the army during the War of 1812 but later deserted. The date and place of his death are unknown.

John Newman

Pennsylvania-born John Newman was arguably the most controversial of the Illinois country recruits. An impetuous young man who enjoyed the dubious distinction of being the only Illinois volunteer to be court-martialed and expelled from the expedition. Newman's disgrace was all the more ironic in light of the fact that Newman, on June 13, 1804, had served as a member of the court that convicted John Collins of being drunk while on sentinel duty and had sentenced him to receive 25 lashes on his back for four consecutive days.

Clark's journal entry for October 12, 1804 noted that Newman and Moses Reed had been confined to camp for uttering criminal and mutinous comments. A court martial convened the following day. Newman was convicted, sentenced to receive 75 lashes and expelled from the Corps of Discovery. He received his lashes on October 14.

Newman's remorse for his rash statements was underscored by his behavior at Fort Mandan. A journal entry dated January 10, 1805 observed that Newman's desire to make himself useful to the expedition during the bitterly cold winter had caused him to spend too much time outside. His hands and feet had frozen, and he suffered extreme pain for several weeks.

Newman pleaded with the commanders not to force him to leave the Corps of Discovery, but to no avail. He was returned to St. Louis in the spring of 1805.

In a letter dated January 15, 1807 to Henry Dearborn, Lewis mentioned that Newman's conduct during his voyage to St. Louis had been commendable. He had served as a hunter and, on several occasions, the boat owed its safety to Newman. Lewis recommended that Newman be given a sum of money that would be deducted from a gratuity awarded to a Frenchman who occupied Newman's position during the latter part of the expedition.

Newman's life after the expedition remains a mystery. The place and date of his death are unknown.

5

Kaskaskia

After departing from Fort Massac with these volunteers, Lewis and Clark went to Kaskaskia for five days to recruit additional men. Founded in 1703 - the second oldest European settlement in Illinois after Cahokia - the village of Kaskaskia was an important site on the Mississippi River's fur trade, and the town prospered. It boasted fine houses, and its inhabitants dressed fashionably. Kaskaskia acquired a reputation as an outpost of French culture and was referred to as the Paris of the West.

Fort Kaskaskia, built in 1703 from lumber and earth, had figured prominently in American history. In 1778 George Rogers Clark, the older brother of William Clark, had occupied the ungarrisoned British posts at Kaskaskia. Captain Russell Bissell commanded Kaskaskia in 1803. Captain Amos Stoddard's artillery company was stationed there as well.

The explorers obtained the majority of their Illinois recruits at Fort Kaskaskia: six volunteers from Bissell's company and five from the company of Stoddard. These men were Sergeant John Ordway and Private Patrick Gass, who later became a sergeant. Other Kaskaskia men included the following privates: John Collins, Peter Weiser, Alexander Willard, Richard Windsor, John Robertson, Isaac White, Ebenezer Tuttle, John Boley and John Dame.

6

John Ordway

Born in Dumbarton, New Hampshire about 1775, John Ordway's journal of the expedition was lost for over a hundred years. It was finally published in 1916.

Ordway was one of the most capable of all the Illinois volunteers, a fact demonstrated by the degree of responsibility and trust that Lewis and Clark delegated to him. He kept the roster and orderly book. As third in command, he was in charge of Camp River Dubois when Lewis and Clark were absent.

Ordway possessed an earthy sense of humor, which was quite evident in a letter to his brother dated September 5, 1803 and mailed while he was still stationed at Kaskaskia. He denied any report that he was engaged to a Miss Nevens and referred to a letter from Betsey Crosby, who was evidently an old flame.

The prospective Illinois volunteer told his brother that he had no desire for Betsey to lose an opportunity to marry someone else by waiting for him. Still, he continued, if she could only remain celibate until his return, he might yet join hands with her.

Ordway's amorous adventures by no means ended when he traveled with the Corps of Discovery. His relationship with a Native American woman incurred the wrath of her jealous husband, and Clark had to intervene. His journal reveals incidents that flesh out the Corps of Discovery and bring its members to life for the modern reader. For instance, his entry for August 16, 1804 noted that the men were in high spirits that day after fiddling and dancing the previous night.

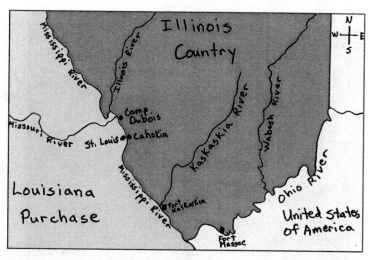

Map of the Illinois Country at he time of Lewis and Clark. (left photo) The confluence of the Ohio and Wabach Rivers in southern Illinois. (right photo) Shawnee National Forest in southern Illinois on the Ohio River.

I

(top photo) An original building from the 1700's, located at Fort Massac Historic Site in southern Illinois. (bottom photo) Fort Kaskaskia, where Lewis and Clark recruited the majority of their Illinois volunteers, was located at this site.

II

Middle photos depict the front and back of Holy Family Church in Cahokia, Illinois. The church was built in 1699 as a mission to the region's Native Americans. Top and bottom photos capture the rustic elegance of the Cahokia Courthouse. It was the westernmost Post Office and Courthouse in the United States at the time of Lewis and Clark. Lewis even mailed a letter from this courthouse to President Thomas Jefferson.

The exterior and interior of a log cabin at the recreated Camp River Dubois in Wood River, Illinois.

The sun peers over a log cabin at the recreated Camp River Dubois in Wood River, Illinois. The cabin's logs have been meticulously joined together in the pioneer manner. Fireplaces provided heat for Lewis and Clark's men during their winter stay at Camp River Dubois. A generous supply of kindling kept cold weather at bay. Firewood was hauled into camp on sleds constructed by Illinois volunteer Patrick Gass. Cabins at the recreated Camp River Dubois have been built close together, just as they were at the time of Lewis and Clark. Cabins at the original Camp River Dubois would have contained windows such as this one.

Panoramic view of the keelboat replica, which
is on display at the Lewis and Clark Interpretive
Center in Hartford, Illinois. The 55-foot keelboat sported 22 oars and one large squaresail.
Two blunderbusses - heavy shotguns that fired
buckshot - were mounted on swivels at the
keelboat's stern.

The keelboat replica at the Lewis and Clark Interpretive Center in Hartford, Illinois is a cutaway model so that visitors can see areas of the boat that were used for various storage purposes. The lids of the storage lockers could be raised to form a breastwork for defense. When the lids were down, they provided catwalks for men with poles pushing the boat. The bow of the keelboat has a small cannon mounted on a swivel. This "swivel gun" could fire a one-pound lead ball or sixteen musket balls.

The Mississippi River as seen from the shore at Hartford, Illinois. The journey of the Corps of Discovery began on this mighty river.

His entry for Christmas Day 1804 remarked that the volunteers enjoyed a Yuletide dinner from the best food that was available to them. After asking the Native Americans not to disturb them on this "great medicine"day, the men danced and fired their guns with abandon.

According to Ordway's journal, the men fired the swivel gun to celebrate New Year's Day 1805 and then went to dance at the Mandan village. Ordway wrote that the volunteers brought along a fiddle, tambourine and sounder horn to provide music.

Ordway also recorded incidents far removed from merriment. On June 29, 1805, he and some other volunteers were caught in a hailstorm. On that day the men had been wearing few clothes because of the extreme heat, and the large hailstones tore into their flesh. He noted that one man had been almost killed, another knocked down and the men without hats were left with bleeding heads.

His journal also gives the reader insights into the folk beliefs of the Native Americans as well as the members of the Corps of Discovery. An entry for August 25, 1804 mentioned the Native Americans telling the explorers about a hill called Hill of the Little Devils that was supposedly inhabited by little people with large heads who would riddle with arrows anyone who ventured there.

Ordway, Lewis, Clark and a party of other men went to the mouth of what Ordway called the "White Stone River" or "Little People River" (now known as the Vermillion River) and then walked three miles from the Missouri to reach the Hill of the Little Devils (now known as Spirit Mound in Clay County, South Dakota). Ordway noted that the party saw a great flock of white birds flying around the hilltop but found no little people on the hill.

Upon meeting Native Americans in present-day Montana, Ordway wrote in his journal that their light complexions and what he thought was a "brogue" in their speech might indicate that they were Welsh-descended Native Americans. Such a supposition seems preposterous today, but Ordway's conjecture must be placed within the context of the times.

Many eighteenth and nineteenth-century Europeans and European-descended Americans earnestly believed that Prince Madoc, a twelfth-century Welsh nobleman had sailed from that country with ten ships of followers. By following contiguous waterways, this band of Celts supposedly had entered the heartland of North America.

Their descendants were thought to have survived as a Native American tribe that retained some Welsh traits, such as the "brogue" to which Ordway referred. Of course, this theory possessed no historical basis, but Ordway's belief in it was not at all unusual for that era.

Ordway also wrote of the Corps of Discovery's return to Camp River Dubois on September 23, 1806. He mentioned that the explorers found a widow who had been there when they departed, noting she had a plantation in the area that was doing reasonably well.

His final journal entry is among the most poignant in any explorers' accounts of the expedition. He wrote that everyone looked forward to boarding in town while awaiting their settlement and then returning home to see their parents from whom they had been so long separated.

Ordway indeed visited his parents upon returning from his service to the Corps of Discovery. He eventually settled in Tywappity Bottom in southeastern Missouri where he cultivated at least two plantations that included peach and apple orchards. He died in Missouri in 1817.

Patrick Gass

Patrick Gass was born in Falling Springs, Pennsylvania on June 12, 1771. His father moved the family to Maryland when Patrick was four, the first of many relocations. Despite Patrick's claim that the sum total of his formal education amounted to just 19 days, he knew how to read, write and cypher.

Gass's father was drafted in 1792 to defend settlers from Native American attacks, but young Patrick willingly took his place in the army. He fought no battles but became acquainted with frontier scouts, who whetted his appetite for travel and adventure.

Two years later, Gass bound himself out as a carpenter's apprentice and became an accomplished craftsman. When war with France seemed imminent, Gass enlisted in the army and reenlisted after his discharge. As a member of Captain Russell Bissell's company, Gass was stationed at Fort Kaskaskia when Lewis arrived looking for volunteers.

Bissell was reluctant to lose such a skilled carpenter, but Gass persisted in his desire to join the Corps of Discovery and requested that Lewis intervene with Bissell on his behalf. At 33, Gass became one of the oldest members of the expedition.

Gass left Kaskaskia as a private but became a sergeant while serving with the Corps of Discovery. When Sergeant Charles Floyd died on August 20, 1804, his fellow volunteers chose Gass by popular vote to replace him.

Gass's carpentry skills were put to good use by Lewis and Clark. He planned the construction of Camp River Dubois and Fort Mandan. Gass also built the canoes for leaving Mandan in spring of 1805 and the canoes to descend the Clearwater at the Nez Perce village in the fall of 1805. He constructed Fort Clatsop in December of that year.

His responsibilities encompassed more than carpentry, however. During the trial in 1804 of John Collins, who was convicted of being drunk while on guard duty, Gass served as a member of the court martial that sentenced Collins to receive 100 lashes. Later that year, Gass also served on the court martial of John Newman.

Gass's journal was published in 1807, the first book to describe the expedition. It remains a valuable chronicle because he recorded details that the other explorers tended to ignore or gloss over. For instance, he was surprisingly frank in mentioning the social interaction between members of the expedition and female Native Americans.

Gass settled in Wellsburg, Virginia - now West Virginia - after his service with the Corps of Discovery. He returned to the army during the War of 1812 and was discharged three years later. During his term of service, he was court martialed twice for being drunk. Gass consumed prodigious amounts of alcohol throughout his life.

In 1831 at age 59, he married 16-year-old Maria Hamilton by whom he had seven children. Maria died in 1847 from measles. All of the children survived to adulthood, except the first child who died at eight months.

He applied to Congress in 1851 for a pension, noting his service to the United States as a member of the Corps of Discovery and a veteran of the War of 1812. His pension petition emphasized that he was a widower with a large family solely dependent on him.

The petition also stressed that Gass had lost an eye during the Battle of Lundy's Lane during the War of 1812. His discharge papers of 1815 stated that Gass had lost his left eye in 1813 due to an injury sustained at Fort Independence on the Mississippi River, in the Missouri Territory.

Despite this fraudulent claim, Gass demonstrated his love for the United States and thirst for adventure when he attempted to volunteer for service in the Union Army at the beginning of the Civil War in 1861. He was 90 years old at the time.

A year later, Gass attended a dinner given in honor of a Union army lieutenant and was toasted as a distinguished veteran. The speaker expressed hope that the 91-year old Gass would live to see the divided nation reunited and free. Gass responded by saying that he hoped the American eagle never lost a feather.

At some point in his old age, Gass posed for an ambrotype, an early type of photograph made by imaging a negative on glass backed by a dark surface. He and Alexander Willard were the only two members of the expedition to be photographed.

Gass died on April 2, 1870 at age 99. He outlived every other member of the Corps of Discovery.

8

John Collins

Born in Frederick County, Maryland, John Collins enjoyed a reputation as one of the best hunters with the Corps of Discovery. His wayward nature, however, tainted even this talent. At Camp River Dubois, Clark referred to Collins as a blackguard because he had evidently killed a farmer's pig and then tried to pass it off as bear meat! Clark's journal entry for New Year's Eve 1803 noted that Collins, along with Alexander Willard and two other recruits, was drunk.

Collins further disgraced himself when the expedition stopped at St. Charles after leaving Camp River Dubois. Along with three other volunteers, Collins went AWOL. After finally returning to the keelboat, he further compounded his problems by making unfavorable remarks about Clark's orders. A court martial sentenced him to 25 lashes on his bare back.

Later during the expedition, Ordway discovered Collins drunk while on sentry duty. A court martial held on June 29, 1804 found him guilty, and he was sentenced to receive 25 lashes for four consecutive days. Despite his sore back, Collins still had to row the keelboat.

Upon completion of the expedition, Collins sold his land warrant to George Drouillard. One source reports that he was killed during a battle with the Arikara tribe on June 2, 1823, while another has him living in St. Louis and dying before 1823.

9

Peter Weiser

Born in Pennsylvania on October 3, 1781, Peter Weiser served the Corps of Discovery as a quartermaster, cook and hunter. Like several of the Illinois recruits, he demonstrated his rebellious nature quite early. Weiser was one of the four men specifically cited by Lewis in his March 3, 1804 Detachment Order as forbidden to leave Camp River Dubois under any circumstances because he and his companions had visited whiskey shops under the pretext of hunting.

Weiser's competence as a hunter and cook during the expedition, however, were later rewarded. Lewis' journal notation for May 18, 1805 mentioned that the Corps honored Weiser by naming a creek after him. The town of Weiser, Idaho and the Weiser River in that state are named for this volunteer.

In August of that year, Weiser became seriously ill with a malady that Lewis described in his journal as colic. The commander gave Weiser a dose of essence of peppermint that had been combined with water as well as some laudanum, an opium derivative that was commonly used in those days for pain relief. Weiser's condition quickly improved, and Lewis let him ride his horse while he walked to camp.

Weiser's experiences with the Corps of Discovery left him with a desire to return to the West. He joined Manuel Lisa's 1807 party to the Upper Missouri and spent time at Fort Lisa. In July 1808, he was one of three men who executed a note for $424.50, which was payable to Lisa. He also spent time exploring and trapping on the Three Forks of the Upper Missouri and the Snake River. He was reported killed sometime during the 1820s.

10

Alexander Willard

Born in 1778 at Charlestown, New Hampshire, Alexander Willard was listed in military records as a blacksmith who enlisted in the army in 1800. He utilized this skill in the Corps of Discovery in addition to serving as a gunsmith and hunter. Willard was also remembered, however, as the recipient of the most horrendous punishment meted out to a member of the expedition.

On the night of July 11-12, 1804, Willard was discovered by Ordway to be asleep while on sentry duty. Unlike other courts convened during the course of the expedition, the members of the court trying Willard consisted only of Lewis and Clark. U.S. Army regulations at that time stipulated the death penalty for such an offense. Even if he were not given a death sentence, Willard knew his conviction would carry a severe penalty.

Willard pled guilty to lying down while on guard duty, but not guilty to being asleep. Lewis and Clark weighed the evidence and then passed judgement: guilty on both charges. They sentenced him to receive 100 lashes on his bare back each day for four days, with the first whipping to occur that day at sunset.

Willard's negligence while on guard duty that night evidently didn't compel the other men to distrust him. Upon the death of Sergeant Floyd, Lewis and Clark allowed the recruits to nominate men for Floyd's position. The men nominated Willard, along with Gass and another man. Gass received 19 votes and was declared the winner, but the fact that Willard was at least nominated demonstrated that the men possessed confidence in him.

On June 18, 1804 Willard was pursued by a grizzly bear that, according to Lewis, almost caught him. He ran into camp followed by the grizzly, which was run off through the efforts of the other men - but not before the bear chased one volunteer into the nearby river!

Willard, along with Peter Weiser, made salt for the party when the expedition reached the west coast. He also obtained blubber from a beached whale, which the explorers thought tasted something like beaver.

While Willard and another expedition member were hunting and exploring, they spent the night with some Chinooks who stole their rifles. Lewis and a party of recruits confronted the Chinooks and threatened them until they returned the rifles.

Like several other members of the expedition, Willard had a creek named for him. The creek, which entered the Beaverhead River, sixty years later was renamed Grasshopper Creek during the gold rush in that area.

Willard worked as a blacksmith in Missouri after leaving the army, but he reenlisted to fight in the War of 1812. After living in the Midwest, Willard and his family migrated by covered wagon to California in 1852. He was fond of boasting in his later years that his fine physique as a young man enabled him to pass the rigorous inspection for fitness to serve in the Corps of Discovery. He said that more than 100 other prospective volunteers had failed the inspection.

Willard died in 1865. At some time in his old age, Willard and his wife, Eleanor, posed for a photograph. It and Gass's ambrotype are the only known photographs of any members of the Corps of Discovery.

11

Richard Windsor

While Richard Windsor's place and date of birth remains unknown, military records show that he enlisted in the army while living in Kentucky. He served on Collins's court martial.

Windsor's good conduct and usefulness during the expedition prompted the commanders to name a creek Windsor's Creek, although the stream was later renamed Cow Creek. He was a member of a party selected by Clark to take the expedition's horses to the Mandan village for use as barter to persuade some of the Mandan chiefs to accompany the expedition back to St. Louis.

This mission to the Mandan tribe proved to be a disaster. While Windsor and the others slept, some Native Americans of the Crow tribe stole their horses. Alone and on foot, the men made two bullboats (boats made from the skins of bull buffalos) and floated down the Yellowstone River to rejoin Clark.

One night during the expedition's return journey, a large wolf entered the camp and attacked the sleeping men. It bit through the hand of one man and then attempted to seize Windsor. A third recruit shot the animal.

Windsor's most hazardous experience with the Corps of Discovery, however, occurred during the journey westward on June 7, 1805 when he and Lewis slipped on a ledge. Lewis quickly regained his footing but heard Windsor pleading for help and asking what should he do. Lewis turned and saw Windsor lying on his stomach with his right arm and leg dangling over the precipice. It was about a 90-foot drop to the river below.

Lewis, although alarmed for Windsor's safety, outwardly

remained calm and assured the young man that he was in no real danger. He advised Windsor to remove his knife with his right hand and dig a foothold for his right foot. Windsor followed Lewis's directions and was able to raise himself to his knees.

The commander then told Windsor to remove his moccasins and come forward on his hands and knees while holding his knife in one hand and rifle in the other. Windsor did exactly as he was told and escaped danger. The two celebrated Windsor's brush with death by feasting on some choice venison.

Windsor settled in Missouri after completing his service with the Corp of Discovery but later re-enlisted in the army. He lived on the Sangamon River in Illinois from 1825 to 1829. The place and date of his death are unknown.

12 *John Robertson*

A native of New Hampshire, John Robertson's date of birth is uncertain. It is thought to have been around 1780. He was a shoemaker by occupation.

Robertson was one of the four volunteers who were confined to Camp River Dubois for ten days by orders of Lewis for visiting whiskey shops while supposedly hunting. He was dismissed from the expedition on June 12, 1804 and ordered to return to St. Louis. Robertson probably rejoined his old company at Kaskaskia: Captain Amos Stoddard's artillery.

Little is known about Robertson's subsequent life, but it is believed that for the next forty years he worked as a fur trader. There are at least two clues concerning his whereabouts.

Robertson sent his mother, who then lived in Owens Station, Missouri, a letter dated August 3, 1837 and mailed from Green River, Wyoming. He told her that he had intended to come home but had just entered into a new fur-trading partnership. A letter dated May 24, 1849 from a man at Fort John - later known as Fort Laramie - stated that Robertson was there. Robertson's date and place of death are uncertain.

13

Isaac White and
Eberezer Tuttle

Born in Holliston, Massachusetts in 1777, Isaac White's military records listed this Illinois volunteer's occupation as a laborer. He was one of the expedition's members who concluded his service at Fort Mandan and returned to St. Louis. The date and place of White's death are uncertain.

Ebenezer Tuttle was born in 1774 in New Haven, Connecticut. He was a farmer prior to this military service and was also returned to St. Louis from Fort Mandan. The date and place of Tuttle's death are also uncertain.

14

John Boley and John Dame

The Pennsylvania-born John Boley was one of the four high-spirited recruits that were confined to Camp River Dubois for ten days for patronizing whiskey shops. He also returned to St. Louis from Fort Mandan.

Although Boley's service with the Corps of Discovery was cut short, he later played a significant role in western exploration. He accompanied Zeb Pike in 1805 on an expedition to the sources of the Mississippi River. A year later, he rejoined Pike for an expedition to the Rocky Mountains. In 1807, another party that included Boley descended the Arkansas River.

Boley and his wife were reported residing in Carondelet, Missouri in 1823. His date and place of death are uncertain.

Born in 1784 in Pallingham, New Hampshire, John Dame was a laborer prior to his military service. He returned to St. Louis from Fort Mandan.

Dame's only mention in any of the journals noted that he killed a pelican while the party was ascending the Missouri. His life after the expedition remains obscure.

15 *Cahokia*

After obtaining these volunteers, the Lewis and Clark party left Kaskaskia for its next destination: the village of Cahokia.

On December 7, 1803 the Lewis and Clark party landed at the mouth of Cahokia Creek, located about three-fourths of a mile from the village of Cahokia. Founded in 1699 as a mission to the region's Native Americans, the village's Holy Family Church was built that same year. It was quite possible that Lewis, Clark and other members of the Corps of Discovery attended a service at Holy Family Church during their time at Cahokia.

Cahokia was the oldest French settlement in the Illinois country and, in 1803, it had a population of 700. From Cahokia, one could see St. Louis, another French settlement located about two and one-half miles away across the Mississippi.

Lewis traveled to St. Louis in an attempt to secure passports from the city's Spanish authorities, which would enable the explorers to journey into the western interior. His request was refused because of Spain's fear that such an expedition would offend other European nations. However, French and British passports had already been obtained before his departure from Washington. Lewis returned to the Illinois country to establish a winter camp for his men.

16 *Camp DuBois*

Lewis selected a site located on 400 acres of land owned by Nicholas Jarrot of Cahokia, a wealthy fur trader. The camp would be established at the mouth of a small river called Dubois - in English, the Wood River. At that time, the mouth of the Dubois was located opposite the mouth of the Missouri River. The site became the Corp of Discovery's Camp River Dubois.

In a letter mailed from Cahokia's U.S. Federal Court House dated December 19, 1803, Lewis informed President Jefferson that he had selected a sufficient number of men at Kaskaskia to complete his party. Some historians believe that Lewis might have been deliberately ambiguous regarding the number of volunteers he had recruited at Kaskaskia. Dearborn's mandate had limited him to no more than 12 non-commissioned officers and privates, and he had far exceeded that number. After rowing up the Mississippi, he realized that a mere dozen men would not be anywhere near enough to complete the expedition.

Lewis spent time in Cahokia and St. Louis as he gathered maps as well as all available information about the territory the Corps of Discovery would enter in the spring of 1804. Clark remained at Camp River Dubois to prepare for the journey.

Clark organized the volunteers into groups with specific daily duties such as blacksmithing, preparing the boats and gathering supplies for the long journey in the spring. Firewood had to be hauled into camp on sleds constructed by Gass. Sergeant John Ordway took charge of the camp during the absence of both Lewis and Clark.

A hunting party left Camp River Dubois daily to keep the men supplied with fresh meat. The volunteers enjoyed a steady diet of deer, turkey, badger, wildcat, wild hog and other game. This high-protein diet was supplemented by area residents, who brought butter and vegetables to Camp River Dubois as gifts or items for barter.

Lewis and Clark knew that the journey westward was fraught with danger. The volunteers at Camp River Dubois were drilled daily in rifle marksmanship and sometimes held shooting competitions with neighboring residents.

The Corps would go west with that era's state of the art weaponry: the air gun. Purchased from Philadelphia gunsmith Isaiah Lukens, the air gun was a pneumatic rifle. The stock served as the reservoir and could be pumped with air to a maximum pressure of six hundred pounds per square inch.

The keelboat used for the journey would also sport some impressive weaponry. Its bow had a small cannon mounted on a swivel. This "swivel gun," as it was called in the explorers' journals, could fire a one-pound lead ball or sixteen musket balls. Clark asked Lewis to acquire four blunderbusses - heavy shotguns that fired buckshot - to provide additional firepower. Lewis obtained the blunderbusses in St. Louis and had two mounted on swivels at the keelboat's stern.

The other two blunderbusses were placed on swivels in the two pirogues that would also be used for traversing the waterways. These pirogues were essentially smaller versions of the keelboat. One had seven oars, the other only six.

The 55-foot keelboat sported 22 oars and carried one large squaresail. Clark modified the keelboat, most notably by having lockers placed along the sides of the boat. The lids of the lockers could be raised to form a breastwork for defense. When the lids were down, they provided catwalks for men with poles pushing the boat. Clark also had eleven three-foot long benches built for the oarsmen.

Much of the work to modify the keelboat was done at Camp River Dubois. Despite the many tasks that had to be performed, the high-spirited Illinois volunteers and the other young recruits at the camp still found time to engage in infractions of military discipline. In a brief note dated January 6, 1804, Clark mentioned disciplining men who fought, became drunk and neglected their duties. He punished the men by ordering them to build a hut for a local woman who had promised to do their washing and sewing.

Detachment orders written by Lewis and dated March 3, 1804 deplore the behavior of some of the men who failed to obey the orders of Sergeant Ordway when both commanders were away from camp. Lewis also reprimanded those men who left Camp River Dubois to visit neighboring whiskey shops under the pretext of hunting or attending to some other business.

The detachment order specifically cited the conduct of four men - including Weiser, Boley and Robertson - for this abuse and forbade them to leave the camp under any pretext for ten days after the order was read aloud to all the volunteers. The order concluded with praise for Ordway's behavior and another admonition to all the volunteers that they were to obey explicitly the orders of Ordway in the absence of the commanding officers.

One might conclude from this episode that Lewis and Clark disapproved of drinking and would have preferred volunteers who were teetotalers. Not at all! The commanders gave their volunteers a gill (four ounces) of whiskey as a reward for good conduct and work well done. Winners of marksmanship competitions were also awarded a gill of whiskey. Weiser, Boley, Robertson and the other man were disciplined for neglecting their duties, not for alcohol consumption per se.

Ordway's letter to his parents, dated April 8, 1804 and written at Camp River Dubois, expressed his excitement upon being granted the opportunity to embark on such a daring expedition into the little-known western country. He told them that he was well and in high spirits at the camp and joyfully noted that he would receive a generous reward upon his return: $15 per month and 400 acres of good land.

However, Ordway's enthusiasm in this letter was tempered by his knowledge that the expedition was undoubtedly hazardous. He informed his parents that fear of accidents incurred while serving with the Corps of Discovery induced him to leave $200 in cash at Kaskaskia, which he asked his parents to invest for him. Ordway also reminded them that, should he not return, his heirs could receive his pay by applying to the government.

While life for the volunteers at Camp River Dubois probably alternated between boredom and rowdiness, there is no reason to believe that it was particularly dangerous. For decades there has been a myth in the region surrounding the location of the camp that at least two members of the Corps of Discovery died during the winter of 1803-04 and were buried in what is now the Milton Cemetery in Alton.

Articles published in The (Alton, IL) Telegraph and Wood River (IL) Journal during the 1950s alluded to this belief. It was also referred to in W.D. Armstrong's A Condensed History of Madison County (Alton, Illinois: National Printing Company, circa 1925) as well as George Thomas Palmer's Historic Landmarks Along the Highways of Illinois (Illinois State Historical Transactions, Publication 39, 1932). Palmer attributed the deaths to bilious fever.

Scholars believe this notion must be consigned to the realm of folklore. There is no mention of a single death at Camp River Dubois in Clark's field notes, and it is difficult to believe that he would have failed to record such a tragic occurrence. Except for an occasional illness or inebriation, all the volunteers probably echoed Ordway's sentiments of being well and in high spirits.

After enduring six months of cramped quarters, the men of the Corps of Discovery welcomed their departure from Camp River Dubois on May 14, 1804. Whitehouse wrote in his journal that, despite a heavy rain, a number of residents from the Goshen settlement, which included the present-day Illinois cities of Edwardsville and Collinsville, came to watch their departure. They fired the swivel gun, hoisted sail and started out in high spirits for their western expedition. The adventure had finally begun.

BIBLIOGRAPHY

Ambrose, Stephen E. *Undaunted Courage: Thomas Jefferson, Meriwether Lewis and the Opening of the American West.* New York: Simon and Schuster, 1996.

Chuinard, Eldon G. *Only One Man Died: The Medical Aspects of the Lewis and Clark Expedition.* Glendale, California: The Arthur H. Clarke Company, 1979.

Clarke, Charles G. *The Men of the Lewis and Clark Expedition.* Lincoln: University of Nebraska Press; Bison Books edition, 2002.

Davis, James E. *Frontier Illinois.* Bloomington: Indiana University Press, 1998.

DeVoto, Bernard, ed. *The Journals of Lewis and Clark.* New York: Houghton Mifflin Company; Mariner Books, 1953, copyright renewed 1981.

Hartley, Robert E. *Lewis and Clark in the Illinois Country.* Westminster, Colorado: Sniktau and Xlibris Publications, 2002.

Jackson, Donald, ed. *Letters of the Lewis and Clark Expedition with Related Documents 1783-1854.* Urbana: University of Illinois Press, 1962.

MacGregor, Carl Lynn, ed. *The Journals of Patrick Gass.* Missoula, Montana: Mountain Press Publishing Company, 1997.

Moulton, Gary, ed. *The Journals of the Lewis and Clark Expedition.* Lincoln: University of Nebraska Press, 1988.

Quaife, Milo M. *The Journals of Captain Meriwether and John Ordway, Kept on the Expedition of Western Exploration, 1803-1806.* Madison: The State Historical Society of Wisconsin, 1965.

Skarsten, M.O. *George Drouillard: Hunter and Interpreter for Lewis and Clark and Fur Trader, 1807-1810, Western Frontiersmen Series XI.* Glendale, California: The Arthur H. Clarke Company, 1964.

Thwaites, Reuben Gold, ed. *Original Journals of the Lewis and Clark Expedition, 1804-1806,* New York: Antiquarian Press LTD, 1959.

Walton, Clyde C. *An Illinois Reader.* DeKalb: Northern Illinois University Press, 1970.